VEHICLE MAINTENANCE LOG BOOK

OWNER INFORMATION

- Name /
- Phone /
- Email /
- Address /

EMERGENCY CONTACT

- Name /
- Phone /

VEHICLE INFORMATION

- License Plate /
- VIN /
- Year-Make-Model /
- Reg. Month /
- Engine Oil Type /
- Purchase Date /
- Purchase Price /
- Purchase ODO /
- Purchase Location /

INSURANCE INFORMATION

- Company /
- Agent /
- Policy # /
- Phone /

CONTENTS

003 - 105
MAINTENANCE LOG
+1300 rows for longterm tracking

106 - 110
ACCIDENT CHECKLIST & LOG
Breathe easy steps ... just in case

Date	ODO	Oil Change	Rotate Tires	Replace Tires	Alignment	Cabin Air Filter	Engine Air Filter	Wiper Blades	Headlights / Taillights	Spark Plugs	BATTERY	Belts & Hoses	Brake Service	Suspension Service	Engine Service	Transmission Service	Power Steering Service	Radiator Service	Cost	Autoshop
Details:																				
Details:																				
Details:																				
Details:																				
Details:																				
Details:																				
Details:																				
Details:																				
Details:																				
Details:																				
Details:																				
Details:																				
Details:																				

Date	ODO	Oil Change	Rotate Tires	Replace Tires	Alignment	Cabin Air Filter	Engine Air Filter	Wiper Blades	Headlights / Taillights	Spark Plugs	BATTERY	Belts & Hoses	Brake Service	Suspension Service	Engine Service	Transmission Service	Power Steering Service	Radiator Service	Cost	Autoshop
		Details:																		
		Details:																		
		Details:																		
		Details:																		
		Details:																		
		Details:																		
		Details:																		
		Details:																		
		Details:																		
		Details:																		
		Details:																		
		Details:																		
		Details:																		

Date	ODO	Oil Change	Rotate Tires	Replace Tires	Alignment	Cabin Air Filter	Engine Air Filter	Wiper Blades	Headlights / Taillights	Spark Plugs	BATTERY	Belts & Hoses	Brake Service	Suspension Service	Engine Service	Transmission Service	Power Steering Service	Radiator Service	Cost	Autoshop
		Details:																		
		Details:																		
		Details:																		
		Details:																		
		Details:																		
		Details:																		
		Details:																		
		Details:																		
		Details:																		
		Details:																		
		Details:																		
		Details:																		
		Details:																		

Date	ODO	Oil Change	Rotate Tires	Replace Tires	Alignment	Cabin Air Filter	Engine Air Filter	Wiper Blades	Headlights / Taillights	Spark Plugs	BATTERY	Belts & Hoses	Brake Service	Suspension Service	Engine Service	Transmission Service	Power Steering Service	Radiator Service	Cost	Autoshop
		Details:																		
		Details:																		
		Details:																		
		Details:																		
		Details:																		
		Details:																		
		Details:																		
		Details:																		
		Details:																		
		Details:																		
		Details:																		
		Details:																		
		Details:																		

Date	ODO	Oil Change	Rotate Tires	Replace Tires	Alignment	Cabin Air Filter	Engine Air Filter	Wiper Blades	Headlights / Taillights	Spark Plugs	BATTERY	Belts & Hoses	Brake Service	Suspension Service	Engine Service	Transmission Service	Power Steering Service	Radiator Service	Cost	Autoshop
		Details:																		
		Details:																		
		Details:																		
		Details:																		
		Details:																		
		Details:																		
		Details:																		
		Details:																		
		Details:																		
		Details:																		
		Details:																		
		Details:																		
		Details:																		

Date	ODO	Oil Change	Rotate Tires	Replace Tires	Alignment	Cabin Air Filter	Engine Air Filter	Wiper Blades	Headlights / Taillights	Spark Plugs	BATTERY	Belts & Hoses	Brake Service	Suspension Service	Engine Service	Transmission Service	Power Steering Service	Radiator Service	Cost	Autoshop
		Details:																		
		Details:																		
		Details:																		
		Details:																		
		Details:																		
		Details:																		
		Details:																		
		Details:																		
		Details:																		
		Details:																		
		Details:																		
		Details:																		
		Details:																		

Date	ODO	Oil Change	Rotate Tires	Replace Tires	Alignment	Cabin Air Filter	Engine Air Filter	Wiper Blades	Headlights / Taillights	Spark Plugs	BATTERY	Belts & Hoses	Brake Service	Suspension Service	Engine Service	Transmission Service	Power Steering Service	Radiator Service	Cost	Autoshop
		Details:																		
		Details:																		
		Details:																		
		Details:																		
		Details:																		
		Details:																		
		Details:																		
		Details:																		
		Details:																		
		Details:																		
		Details:																		
		Details:																		
		Details:																		

Date	ODO	Oil Change	Rotate Tires	Replace Tires	Alignment	Cabin Air Filter	Engine Air Filter	Wiper Blades	Headlights / Taillights	Spark Plugs	BATTERY	Belts & Hoses	Brake Service	Suspension Service	Engine Service	Transmission Service	Power Steering Service	Radiator Service	Cost	Autoshop
		Details:																		
		Details:																		
		Details:																		
		Details:																		
		Details:																		
		Details:																		
		Details:																		
		Details:																		
		Details:																		
		Details:																		
		Details:																		
		Details:																		
		Details:																		

Date	ODO	Oil Change	Rotate Tires	Replace Tires	Alignment	Cabin Air Filter	Engine Air Filter	Wiper Blades	Headlights / Taillights	Spark Plugs	BATTERY	Belts & Hoses	Brake Service	Suspension Service	Engine Service	Transmission Service	Power Steering Service	Radiator Service	Cost	Autoshop
		Details:																		
		Details:																		
		Details:																		
		Details:																		
		Details:																		
		Details:																		
		Details:																		
		Details:																		
		Details:																		
		Details:																		
		Details:																		
		Details:																		
		Details:																		

Date	ODO	Oil Change	Rotate Tires	Replace Tires	Alignment	Cabin Air Filter	Engine Air Filter	Wiper Blades	Headlights / Taillights	Spark Plugs	BATTERY	Belts & Hoses	Brake Service	Suspension Service	Engine Service	Transmission Service	Power Steering Service	Radiator Service	Cost	Autoshop
Details:																				
Details:																				
Details:																				
Details:																				
Details:																				
Details:																				
Details:																				
Details:																				
Details:																				
Details:																				
Details:																				
Details:																				
Details:																				

Date	ODO	Oil Change	Rotate Tires	Replace Tires	Alignment	Cabin Air Filter	Engine Air Filter	Wiper Blades	Headlights / Taillights	Spark Plugs	BATTERY	Belts & Hoses	Brake Service	Suspension Service	Engine Service	Transmission Service	Power Steering Service	Radiator Service	Cost	Autoshop
Details:																				
Details:																				
Details:																				
Details:																				
Details:																				
Details:																				
Details:																				
Details:																				
Details:																				
Details:																				
Details:																				
Details:																				
Details:																				

Date	ODO	Oil Change	Rotate Tires	Replace Tires	Alignment	Cabin Air Filter	Engine Air Filter	Wiper Blades	Headlights / Taillights	Spark Plugs	BATTERY	Belts & Hoses	Brake Service	Suspension Service	Engine Service	Transmission Service	Power Steering Service	Radiator Service	Cost	Autoshop
Details:																				
Details:																				
Details:																				
Details:																				
Details:																				
Details:																				
Details:																				
Details:																				
Details:																				
Details:																				
Details:																				
Details:																				
Details:																				

Date	ODO	Oil Change	Rotate Tires	Replace Tires	Alignment	Cabin Air Filter	Engine Air Filter	Wiper Blades	Headlights / Taillights	Spark Plugs	BATTERY	Belts & Hoses	Brake Service	Suspension Service	Engine Service	Transmission Service	Power Steering Service	Radiator Service	Cost	Autoshop

Details:

(repeat 13 rows)

Date	ODO	Oil Change	Rotate Tires	Replace Tires	Alignment	Cabin Air Filter	Engine Air Filter	Wiper Blades	Headlights / Taillights	Spark Plugs	BATTERY	Belts & Hoses	Brake Service	Suspension Service	Engine Service	Transmission Service	Power Steering Service	Radiator Service	Cost	Autoshop

Details:

Details:

Details:

Details:

Details:

Details:

Details:

Details:

Details:

Details:

Details:

Details:

Details:

Date	ODO	Oil Change	Rotate Tires	Replace Tires	Alignment	Cabin Air Filter	Engine Air Filter	Wiper Blades	Headlights / Taillights	Spark Plugs	BATTERY	Belts & Hoses	Brake Service	Suspension Service	Engine Service	Transmission Service	Power Steering Service	Radiator Service	Cost	Autoshop
		Details:																		
		Details:																		
		Details:																		
		Details:																		
		Details:																		
		Details:																		
		Details:																		
		Details:																		
		Details:																		
		Details:																		
		Details:																		
		Details:																		
		Details:																		

Date	ODO	Oil Change	Rotate Tires	Replace Tires	Alignment	Cabin Air Filter	Engine Air Filter	Wiper Blades	Headlights / Taillights	Spark Plugs	BATTERY	Belts & Hoses	Brake Service	Suspension Service	Engine Service	Transmission Service	Power Steering Service	Radiator Service	Cost	Autoshop
		Details:																		
		Details:																		
		Details:																		
		Details:																		
		Details:																		
		Details:																		
		Details:																		
		Details:																		
		Details:																		
		Details:																		
		Details:																		
		Details:																		
		Details:																		

Date	ODO	Oil Change	Rotate Tires	Replace Tires	Alignment	Cabin Air Filter	Engine Air Filter	Wiper Blades	Headlights / Taillights	Spark Plugs	BATTERY	Belts & Hoses	Brake Service	Suspension Service	Engine Service	Transmission Service	Power Steering Service	Radiator Service	Cost	Autoshop
		Details:																		
		Details:																		
		Details:																		
		Details:																		
		Details:																		
		Details:																		
		Details:																		
		Details:																		
		Details:																		
		Details:																		
		Details:																		
		Details:																		
		Details:																		

Date	ODO	Oil Change	Rotate Tires	Replace Tires	Alignment	Cabin Air Filter	Engine Air Filter	Wiper Blades	Headlights / Taillights	Spark Plugs	BATTERY	Belts & Hoses	Brake Service	Suspension Service	Engine Service	Transmission Service	Power Steering Service	Radiator Service	Cost	Autoshop
		Details:																		
		Details:																		
		Details:																		
		Details:																		
		Details:																		
		Details:																		
		Details:																		
		Details:																		
		Details:																		
		Details:																		
		Details:																		
		Details:																		
		Details:																		

Date	ODO	Oil Change	Rotate Tires	Replace Tires	Alignment	Cabin Air Filter	Engine Air Filter	Wiper Blades	Headlights / Taillights	Spark Plugs	BATTERY	Belts & Hoses	Brake Service	Suspension Service	Engine Service	Transmission Service	Power Steering Service	Radiator Service	Cost	Autoshop
		Details:																		
		Details:																		
		Details:																		
		Details:																		
		Details:																		
		Details:																		
		Details:																		
		Details:																		
		Details:																		
		Details:																		
		Details:																		
		Details:																		
		Details:																		

Date	ODO	Oil Change	Rotate Tires	Replace Tires	Alignment	Cabin Air Filter	Engine Air Filter	Wiper Blades	Headlights / Taillights	Spark Plugs	BATTERY	Belts & Hoses	Brake Service	Suspension Service	Engine Service	Transmission Service	Power Steering Service	Radiator Service	Cost	Autoshop

Details:

Details:

Details:

Details:

Details:

Details:

Details:

Details:

Details:

Details:

Details:

Details:

Details:

Details:

Date	ODO	Oil Change	Rotate Tires	Replace Tires	Alignment	Cabin Air Filter	Engine Air Filter	Wiper Blades	Headlights / Taillights	Spark Plugs	BATTERY	Belts & Hoses	Brake Service	Suspension Service	Engine Service	Transmission Service	Power Steering Service	Radiator Service	Cost	Autoshop
		Details:																		
		Details:																		
		Details:																		
		Details:																		
		Details:																		
		Details:																		
		Details:																		
		Details:																		
		Details:																		
		Details:																		
		Details:																		
		Details:																		
		Details:																		

Date	ODO	Oil Change	Rotate Tires	Replace Tires	Alignment	Cabin Air Filter	Engine Air Filter	Wiper Blades	Headlights / Taillights	Spark Plugs	BATTERY	Belts & Hoses	Brake Service	Suspension Service	Engine Service	Transmission Service	Power Steering Service	Radiator Service	Cost	Autoshop
		Details:																		
		Details:																		
		Details:																		
		Details:																		
		Details:																		
		Details:																		
		Details:																		
		Details:																		
		Details:																		
		Details:																		
		Details:																		
		Details:																		
		Details:																		

Date	ODO	Oil Change	Rotate Tires	Replace Tires	Alignment	Cabin Air Filter	Engine Air Filter	Wiper Blades	Headlights / Taillights	Spark Plugs	BATTERY	Belts & Hoses	Brake Service	Suspension Service	Engine Service	Transmission Service	Power Steering Service	Radiator Service	Cost	Autoshop
		Details:																		
		Details:																		
		Details:																		
		Details:																		
		Details:																		
		Details:																		
		Details:																		
		Details:																		
		Details:																		
		Details:																		
		Details:																		
		Details:																		
		Details:																		

Date	ODO	Oil Change	Rotate Tires	Replace Tires	Alignment	Cabin Air Filter	Engine Air Filter	Wiper Blades	Headlights / Taillights	Spark Plugs	BATTERY	Belts & Hoses	Brake Service	Suspension Service	Engine Service	Transmission Service	Power Steering Service	Radiator Service	Cost	Autoshop
		Details:																		
		Details:																		
		Details:																		
		Details:																		
		Details:																		
		Details:																		
		Details:																		
		Details:																		
		Details:																		
		Details:																		
		Details:																		
		Details:																		
		Details:																		

Date	ODO	Oil Change	Rotate Tires	Replace Tires	Alignment	Cabin Air Filter	Engine Air Filter	Wiper Blades	Headlights / Taillights	Spark Plugs	BATTERY	Belts & Hoses	Brake Service	Suspension Service	Engine Service	Transmission Service	Power Steering Service	Radiator Service	Cost	Autoshop

Details:

Details:

Details:

Details:

Details:

Details:

Details:

Details:

Details:

Details:

Details:

Details:

Details:

Date	ODO	Oil Change	Rotate Tires	Replace Tires	Alignment	Cabin Air Filter	Engine Air Filter	Wiper Blades	Headlights / Taillights	Spark Plugs	BATTERY	Belts & Hoses	Brake Service	Suspension Service	Engine Service	Transmission Service	Power Steering Service	Radiator Service	Cost	Autoshop
		Details:																		
		Details:																		
		Details:																		
		Details:																		
		Details:																		
		Details:																		
		Details:																		
		Details:																		
		Details:																		
		Details:																		
		Details:																		
		Details:																		
		Details:																		

Date	ODO	Oil Change	Rotate Tires	Replace Tires	Alignment	Cabin Air Filter	Engine Air Filter	Wiper Blades	Headlights / Taillights	Spark Plugs	BATTERY	Belts & Hoses	Brake Service	Suspension Service	Engine Service	Transmission Service	Power Steering Service	Radiator Service	Cost	Autoshop
		Details:																		
		Details:																		
		Details:																		
		Details:																		
		Details:																		
		Details:																		
		Details:																		
		Details:																		
		Details:																		
		Details:																		
		Details:																		
		Details:																		
		Details:																		

Date	ODO	Oil Change	Rotate Tires	Replace Tires	Alignment	Cabin Air Filter	Engine Air Filter	Wiper Blades	Headlights / Taillights	Spark Plugs	BATTERY	Belts & Hoses	Brake Service	Suspension Service	Engine Service	Transmission Service	Power Steering Service	Radiator Service	Cost	Autoshop
		Details:																		
		Details:																		
		Details:																		
		Details:																		
		Details:																		
		Details:																		
		Details:																		
		Details:																		
		Details:																		
		Details:																		
		Details:																		
		Details:																		
		Details:																		

Date	ODO	Oil Change	Rotate Tires	Replace Tires	Alignment	Cabin Air Filter	Engine Air Filter	Wiper Blades	Headlights / Taillights	Spark Plugs	BATTERY	Belts & Hoses	Brake Service	Suspension Service	Engine Service	Transmission Service	Power Steering Service	Radiator Service	Cost	Autoshop
		Details:																		
		Details:																		
		Details:																		
		Details:																		
		Details:																		
		Details:																		
		Details:																		
		Details:																		
		Details:																		
		Details:																		
		Details:																		
		Details:																		
		Details:																		

Date	ODO	Oil Change	Rotate Tires	Replace Tires	Alignment	Cabin Air Filter	Engine Air Filter	Wiper Blades	Headlights / Taillights	Spark Plugs	BATTERY	Belts & Hoses	Brake Service	Suspension Service	Engine Service	Transmission Service	Power Steering Service	Radiator Service	Cost	Autoshop
Details:																				
Details:																				
Details:																				
Details:																				
Details:																				
Details:																				
Details:																				
Details:																				
Details:																				
Details:																				
Details:																				
Details:																				
Details:																				

Date	ODO	Oil Change	Rotate Tires	Replace Tires	Alignment	Cabin Air Filter	Engine Air Filter	Wiper Blades	Headlights / Taillights	Spark Plugs	BATTERY	Belts & Hoses	Brake Service	Suspension Service	Engine Service	Transmission Service	Power Steering Service	Radiator Service	Cost	Autoshop
		Details:																		
		Details:																		
		Details:																		
		Details:																		
		Details:																		
		Details:																		
		Details:																		
		Details:																		
		Details:																		
		Details:																		
		Details:																		
		Details:																		
		Details:																		

Date	ODO	Oil Change	Rotate Tires	Replace Tires	Alignment	Cabin Air Filter	Engine Air Filter	Wiper Blades	Headlights / Taillights	Spark Plugs	BATTERY	Belts & Hoses	Brake Service	Suspension Service	Engine Service	Transmission Service	Power Steering Service	Radiator Service	Cost	Autoshop
		Details:																		
		Details:																		
		Details:																		
		Details:																		
		Details:																		
		Details:																		
		Details:																		
		Details:																		
		Details:																		
		Details:																		
		Details:																		
		Details:																		
		Details:																		

Date	ODO	Oil Change	Rotate Tires	Replace Tires	Alignment	Cabin Air Filter	Engine Air Filter	Wiper Blades	Headlights / Taillights	Spark Plugs	BATTERY	Belts & Hoses	Brake Service	Suspension Service	Engine Service	Transmission Service	Power Steering Service	Radiator Service	Cost	Autoshop
		Details:																		
		Details:																		
		Details:																		
		Details:																		
		Details:																		
		Details:																		
		Details:																		
		Details:																		
		Details:																		
		Details:																		
		Details:																		
		Details:																		

Date	ODO	Oil Change	Rotate Tires	Replace Tires	Alignment	Cabin Air Filter	Engine Air Filter	Wiper Blades	Headlights / Taillights	Spark Plugs	BATTERY	Belts & Hoses	Brake Service	Suspension Service	Engine Service	Transmission Service	Power Steering Service	Radiator Service	Cost	Autoshop
		Details:																		
		Details:																		
		Details:																		
		Details:																		
		Details:																		
		Details:																		
		Details:																		
		Details:																		
		Details:																		
		Details:																		
		Details:																		
		Details:																		
		Details:																		

Date	ODO	Oil Change	Rotate Tires	Replace Tires	Alignment	Cabin Air Filter	Engine Air Filter	Wiper Blades	Headlights / Taillights	Spark Plugs	BATTERY	Belts & Hoses	Brake Service	Suspension Service	Engine Service	Transmission Service	Power Steering Service	Radiator Service	Cost	Autoshop
		Details:																		
		Details:																		
		Details:																		
		Details:																		
		Details:																		
		Details:																		
		Details:																		
		Details:																		
		Details:																		
		Details:																		
		Details:																		
		Details:																		

Date	ODO	Oil Change	Rotate Tires	Replace Tires	Alignment	Cabin Air Filter	Engine Air Filter	Wiper Blades	Headlights / Taillights	Spark Plugs	BATTERY	Belts & Hoses	Brake Service	Suspension Service	Engine Service	Transmission Service	Power Steering Service	Radiator Service	Cost	Autoshop
		Details:																		
		Details:																		
		Details:																		
		Details:																		
		Details:																		
		Details:																		
		Details:																		
		Details:																		
		Details:																		
		Details:																		
		Details:																		
		Details:																		
		Details:																		

Date	ODO	Oil Change	Rotate Tires	Replace Tires	Alignment	Cabin Air Filter	Engine Air Filter	Wiper Blades	Headlights / Taillights	Spark Plugs	BATTERY	Belts & Hoses	Brake Service	Suspension Service	Engine Service	Transmission Service	Power Steering Service	Radiator Service	Cost	Autoshop
		Details:																		
		Details:																		
		Details:																		
		Details:																		
		Details:																		
		Details:																		
		Details:																		
		Details:																		
		Details:																		
		Details:																		
		Details:																		
		Details:																		
		Details:																		

Date	ODO	Oil Change	Rotate Tires	Replace Tires	Alignment	Cabin Air Filter	Engine Air Filter	Wiper Blades	Headlights / Taillights	Spark Plugs	BATTERY	Belts & Hoses	Brake Service	Suspension Service	Engine Service	Transmission Service	Power Steering Service	Radiator Service	Cost	Autoshop
		Details:																		
		Details:																		
		Details:																		
		Details:																		
		Details:																		
		Details:																		
		Details:																		
		Details:																		
		Details:																		
		Details:																		
		Details:																		
		Details:																		
		Details:																		

Date	ODO	Oil Change	Rotate Tires	Replace Tires	Alignment	Cabin Air Filter	Engine Air Filter	Wiper Blades	Headlights / Taillights	Spark Plugs	BATTERY	Belts & Hoses	Brake Service	Suspension Service	Engine Service	Transmission Service	Power Steering Service	Radiator Service	Cost	Autoshop
		Details:																		
		Details:																		
		Details:																		
		Details:																		
		Details:																		
		Details:																		
		Details:																		
		Details:																		
		Details:																		
		Details:																		
		Details:																		
		Details:																		
		Details:																		

Date	ODO	Oil Change	Rotate Tires	Replace Tires	Alignment	Cabin Air Filter	Engine Air Filter	Wiper Blades	Headlights / Taillights	Spark Plugs	BATTERY	Belts & Hoses	Brake Service	Suspension Service	Engine Service	Transmission Service	Power Steering Service	Radiator Service	Cost	Autoshop
		Details:																		
		Details:																		
		Details:																		
		Details:																		
		Details:																		
		Details:																		
		Details:																		
		Details:																		
		Details:																		
		Details:																		
		Details:																		
		Details:																		

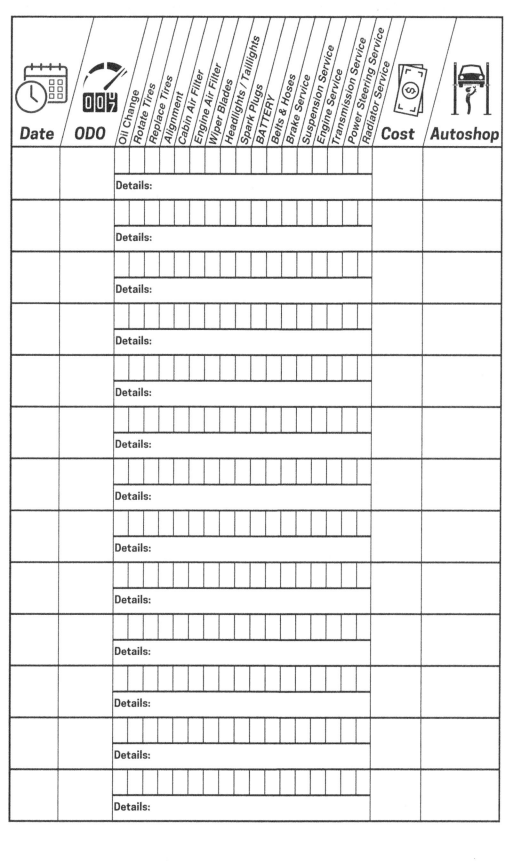

Date	ODO	Oil Change	Rotate Tires	Replace Tires	Alignment	Cabin Air Filter	Engine Air Filter	Wiper Blades	Headlights / Taillights	Spark Plugs	BATTERY	Belts & Hoses	Brake Service	Suspension Service	Engine Service	Transmission Service	Power Steering Service	Radiator Service	Cost	Autoshop
		Details:																		
		Details:																		
		Details:																		
		Details:																		
		Details:																		
		Details:																		
		Details:																		
		Details:																		
		Details:																		
		Details:																		
		Details:																		
		Details:																		
		Details:																		

Date	ODO	Oil Change	Rotate Tires	Replace Tires	Alignment	Cabin Air Filter	Engine Air Filter	Wiper Blades	Headlights / Taillights	Spark Plugs	BATTERY	Belts & Hoses	Brake Service	Suspension Service	Engine Service	Transmission Service	Power Steering Service	Radiator Service	Cost	Autoshop
Details:																				
Details:																				
Details:																				
Details:																				
Details:																				
Details:																				
Details:																				
Details:																				
Details:																				
Details:																				
Details:																				
Details:																				
Details:																				

Date	ODO	Oil Change	Rotate Tires	Replace Tires	Alignment	Cabin Air Filter	Engine Air Filter	Wiper Blades	Headlights / Taillights	Spark Plugs	BATTERY	Belts & Hoses	Brake Service	Suspension Service	Engine Service	Transmission Service	Power Steering Service	Radiator Service	Cost	Autoshop
		Details:																		
		Details:																		
		Details:																		
		Details:																		
		Details:																		
		Details:																		
		Details:																		
		Details:																		
		Details:																		
		Details:																		
		Details:																		
		Details:																		
		Details:																		

Date	ODO	Oil Change	Rotate Tires	Replace Tires	Alignment	Cabin Air Filter	Engine Air Filter	Wiper Blades	Headlights / Taillights	Spark Plugs	BATTERY	Belts & Hoses	Brake Service	Suspension Service	Engine Service	Transmission Service	Power Steering Service	Radiator Service	Cost	Autoshop
Details:																				
Details:																				
Details:																				
Details:																				
Details:																				
Details:																				
Details:																				
Details:																				
Details:																				
Details:																				
Details:																				
Details:																				
Details:																				

Date	ODO	Oil Change	Rotate Tires	Replace Tires	Alignment	Cabin Air Filter	Engine Air Filter	Wiper Blades	Headlights / Taillights	Spark Plugs	BATTERY	Belts & Hoses	Brake Service	Suspension Service	Engine Service	Transmission Service	Power Steering Service	Radiator Service	Cost	Autoshop
		Details:																		
		Details:																		
		Details:																		
		Details:																		
		Details:																		
		Details:																		
		Details:																		
		Details:																		
		Details:																		
		Details:																		
		Details:																		
		Details:																		
		Details:																		

Date	ODO	Oil Change	Rotate Tires	Replace Tires	Alignment	Cabin Air Filter	Engine Air Filter	Wiper Blades	Headlights / Taillights	Spark Plugs	BATTERY	Belts & Hoses	Brake Service	Suspension Service	Engine Service	Transmission Service	Power Steering Service	Radiator Service	Cost	Autoshop
		Details:																		
		Details:																		
		Details:																		
		Details:																		
		Details:																		
		Details:																		
		Details:																		
		Details:																		
		Details:																		
		Details:																		
		Details:																		
		Details:																		
		Details:																		

Date	ODO	Oil Change	Rotate Tires	Replace Tires	Alignment	Cabin Air Filter	Engine Air Filter	Wiper Blades	Headlights / Taillights	Spark Plugs	BATTERY	Belts & Hoses	Brake Service	Suspension Service	Engine Service	Transmission Service	Power Steering Service	Radiator Service	Cost	Autoshop
		Details:																		
		Details:																		
		Details:																		
		Details:																		
		Details:																		
		Details:																		
		Details:																		
		Details:																		
		Details:																		
		Details:																		
		Details:																		
		Details:																		
		Details:																		

Date	ODO	Oil Change	Rotate Tires	Replace Tires	Alignment	Cabin Air Filter	Engine Air Filter	Wiper Blades	Headlights / Taillights	Spark Plugs	BATTERY	Belts & Hoses	Brake Service	Suspension Service	Engine Service	Transmission Service	Power Steering Service	Radiator Service	Cost	Autoshop
		Details:																		
		Details:																		
		Details:																		
		Details:																		
		Details:																		
		Details:																		
		Details:																		
		Details:																		
		Details:																		
		Details:																		
		Details:																		
		Details:																		
		Details:																		

Date	ODO	Oil Change	Rotate Tires	Replace Tires	Alignment	Cabin Air Filter	Engine Air Filter	Wiper Blades	Headlights / Taillights	Spark Plugs	BATTERY	Belts & Hoses	Brake Service	Suspension Service	Engine Service	Transmission Service	Power Steering Service	Radiator Service	Cost	Autoshop
		Details:																		
		Details:																		
		Details:																		
		Details:																		
		Details:																		
		Details:																		
		Details:																		
		Details:																		
		Details:																		
		Details:																		
		Details:																		
		Details:																		
		Details:																		

Date	ODO	Oil Change	Rotate Tires	Replace Tires	Alignment	Cabin Air Filter	Engine Air Filter	Wiper Blades	Headlights / Taillights	Spark Plugs	BATTERY	Belts & Hoses	Brake Service	Suspension Service	Engine Service	Transmission Service	Power Steering Service	Radiator Service	Cost	Autoshop

Details:

Date	ODO	Oil Change	Rotate Tires	Replace Tires	Alignment	Cabin Air Filter	Engine Air Filter	Wiper Blades	Headlights / Taillights	Spark Plugs	BATTERY	Belts & Hoses	Brake Service	Suspension Service	Engine Service	Transmission Service	Power Steering Service	Radiator Service	Cost	Autoshop
		Details:																		
		Details:																		
		Details:																		
		Details:																		
		Details:																		
		Details:																		
		Details:																		
		Details:																		
		Details:																		
		Details:																		
		Details:																		
		Details:																		
		Details:																		

Date	ODO	Oil Change	Rotate Tires	Replace Tires	Alignment	Cabin Air Filter	Engine Air Filter	Wiper Blades	Headlights / Taillights	Spark Plugs	BATTERY	Belts & Hoses	Brake Service	Suspension Service	Engine Service	Transmission Service	Power Steering Service	Radiator Service	Cost	Autoshop
Details:																				
Details:																				
Details:																				
Details:																				
Details:																				
Details:																				
Details:																				
Details:																				
Details:																				
Details:																				
Details:																				
Details:																				
Details:																				

Date	ODO	Oil Change	Rotate Tires	Replace Tires	Alignment	Cabin Air Filter	Engine Air Filter	Wiper Blades	Headlights / Taillights	Spark Plugs	BATTERY	Belts & Hoses	Brake Service	Suspension Service	Engine Service	Transmission Service	Power Steering Service	Radiator Service	Cost	Autoshop
		Details:																		
		Details:																		
		Details:																		
		Details:																		
		Details:																		
		Details:																		
		Details:																		
		Details:																		
		Details:																		
		Details:																		
		Details:																		
		Details:																		
		Details:																		

Date	ODO	Oil Change	Rotate Tires	Replace Tires	Alignment	Cabin Air Filter	Engine Air Filter	Wiper Blades	Headlights / Taillights	Spark Plugs	BATTERY	Belts & Hoses	Brake Service	Suspension Service	Engine Service	Transmission Service	Power Steering Service	Radiator Service	Cost	Autoshop
		Details:																		
		Details:																		
		Details:																		
		Details:																		
		Details:																		
		Details:																		
		Details:																		
		Details:																		
		Details:																		
		Details:																		
		Details:																		
		Details:																		
		Details:																		

Date	ODO	Oil Change	Rotate Tires	Replace Tires	Alignment	Cabin Air Filter	Engine Air Filter	Wiper Blades	Headlights / Taillights	Spark Plugs	BATTERY	Belts & Hoses	Brake Service	Suspension Service	Engine Service	Transmission Service	Power Steering Service	Radiator Service	Cost	Autoshop
		Details:																		
		Details:																		
		Details:																		
		Details:																		
		Details:																		
		Details:																		
		Details:																		
		Details:																		
		Details:																		
		Details:																		
		Details:																		
		Details:																		
		Details:																		

Date	ODO	Oil Change	Rotate Tires	Replace Tires	Alignment	Cabin Air Filter	Engine Air Filter	Wiper Blades	Headlights / Taillights	Spark Plugs	BATTERY	Belts & Hoses	Brake Service	Suspension Service	Engine Service	Transmission Service	Power Steering Service	Radiator Service	Cost	Autoshop
									Details:											
									Details:											
									Details:											
									Details:											
									Details:											
									Details:											
									Details:											
									Details:											
									Details:											
									Details:											
									Details:											
									Details:											
									Details:											

Date	ODO	Oil Change	Rotate Tires	Replace Tires	Alignment	Cabin Air Filter	Engine Air Filter	Wiper Blades	Headlights / Taillights	Spark Plugs	BATTERY	Belts & Hoses	Brake Service	Suspension Service	Engine Service	Transmission Service	Power Steering Service	Radiator Service	Cost	Autoshop
		Details:																		
		Details:																		
		Details:																		
		Details:																		
		Details:																		
		Details:																		
		Details:																		
		Details:																		
		Details:																		
		Details:																		
		Details:																		
		Details:																		
		Details:																		

Date	ODO	Oil Change	Rotate Tires	Replace Tires	Alignment	Cabin Air Filter	Engine Air Filter	Wiper Blades	Headlights / Taillights	Spark Plugs	BATTERY	Belts & Hoses	Brake Service	Suspension Service	Engine Service	Transmission Service	Power Steering Service	Radiator Service	Cost	Autoshop
		Details:																		
		Details:																		
		Details:																		
		Details:																		
		Details:																		
		Details:																		
		Details:																		
		Details:																		
		Details:																		
		Details:																		
		Details:																		
		Details:																		
		Details:																		

Date	ODO	Oil Change	Rotate Tires	Replace Tires	Alignment	Cabin Air Filter	Engine Air Filter	Wiper Blades	Headlights / Taillights	Spark Plugs	BATTERY	Belts & Hoses	Brake Service	Suspension Service	Engine Service	Transmission Service	Power Steering Service	Radiator Service	Cost	Autoshop
Details:																				
Details:																				
Details:																				
Details:																				
Details:																				
Details:																				
Details:																				
Details:																				
Details:																				
Details:																				
Details:																				
Details:																				
Details:																				

Date	ODO	Oil Change	Rotate Tires	Replace Tires	Alignment	Cabin Air Filter	Engine Air Filter	Wiper Blades	Headlights / Taillights	Spark Plugs	BATTERY	Belts & Hoses	Brake Service	Suspension Service	Engine Service	Transmission Service	Power Steering Service	Radiator Service	Cost	Autoshop
		Details:																		
		Details:																		
		Details:																		
		Details:																		
		Details:																		
		Details:																		
		Details:																		
		Details:																		
		Details:																		
		Details:																		
		Details:																		
		Details:																		
		Details:																		

Date	ODO	Oil Change	Rotate Tires	Replace Tires	Alignment	Cabin Air Filter	Engine Air Filter	Wiper Blades	Headlights / Taillights	Spark Plugs	BATTERY	Belts & Hoses	Brake Service	Suspension Service	Engine Service	Transmission Service	Power Steering Service	Radiator Service	Cost	Autoshop

Details:

Details:

Details:

Details:

Details:

Details:

Details:

Details:

Details:

Details:

Details:

Details:

Details:

Date	ODO	Oil Change	Rotate Tires	Replace Tires	Alignment	Cabin Air Filter	Engine Air Filter	Wiper Blades	Headlights / Taillights	Spark Plugs	BATTERY	Belts & Hoses	Brake Service	Suspension Service	Engine Service	Transmission Service	Power Steering Service	Radiator Service	Cost	Autoshop
		Details:																		
		Details:																		
		Details:																		
		Details:																		
		Details:																		
		Details:																		
		Details:																		
		Details:																		
		Details:																		
		Details:																		
		Details:																		
		Details:																		
		Details:																		

Date	ODO	Oil Change	Rotate Tires	Replace Tires	Alignment	Cabin Air Filter	Engine Air Filter	Wiper Blades	Headlights / Taillights	Spark Plugs	BATTERY	Belts & Hoses	Brake Service	Suspension Service	Engine Service	Transmission Service	Power Steering Service	Radiator Service	Cost	Autoshop
		Details:																		
		Details:																		
		Details:																		
		Details:																		
		Details:																		
		Details:																		
		Details:																		
		Details:																		
		Details:																		
		Details:																		
		Details:																		
		Details:																		
		Details:																		

Date	ODO	Oil Change	Rotate Tires	Replace Tires	Alignment	Cabin Air Filter	Engine Air Filter	Wiper Blades	Headlights / Taillights	Spark Plugs	BATTERY	Belts & Hoses	Brake Service	Suspension Service	Engine Service	Transmission Service	Power Steering Service	Radiator Service	Cost	Autoshop
		Details:																		
		Details:																		
		Details:																		
		Details:																		
		Details:																		
		Details:																		
		Details:																		
		Details:																		
		Details:																		
		Details:																		
		Details:																		
		Details:																		
		Details:																		

Date	ODO	Oil Change	Rotate Tires	Replace Tires	Alignment	Cabin Air Filter	Engine Air Filter	Wiper Blades	Headlights / Taillights	Spark Plugs	BATTERY	Belts & Hoses	Brake Service	Suspension Service	Engine Service	Transmission Service	Power Steering Service	Radiator Service	Cost	Autoshop
		Details:																		
		Details:																		
		Details:																		
		Details:																		
		Details:																		
		Details:																		
		Details:																		
		Details:																		
		Details:																		
		Details:																		
		Details:																		
		Details:																		
		Details:																		

Date	ODO	Oil Change	Rotate Tires	Replace Tires	Alignment	Cabin Air Filter	Engine Air Filter	Wiper Blades	Headlights / Taillights	Spark Plugs	BATTERY	Belts & Hoses	Brake Service	Suspension Service	Engine Service	Transmission Service	Power Steering Service	Radiator Service	Cost	Autoshop
		Details:																		
		Details:																		
		Details:																		
		Details:																		
		Details:																		
		Details:																		
		Details:																		
		Details:																		
		Details:																		
		Details:																		
		Details:																		
		Details:																		

Date	ODO	Oil Change	Rotate Tires	Replace Tires	Alignment	Cabin Air Filter	Engine Air Filter	Wiper Blades	Headlights / Taillights	Spark Plugs	BATTERY	Belts & Hoses	Brake Service	Suspension Service	Engine Service	Transmission Service	Power Steering Service	Radiator Service	Cost	Autoshop
		Details:																		
		Details:																		
		Details:																		
		Details:																		
		Details:																		
		Details:																		
		Details:																		
		Details:																		
		Details:																		
		Details:																		
		Details:																		
		Details:																		
		Details:																		

Date	ODO	Oil Change	Rotate Tires	Replace Tires	Alignment	Cabin Air Filter	Engine Air Filter	Wiper Blades	Headlights / Taillights	Spark Plugs	BATTERY	Belts & Hoses	Brake Service	Suspension Service	Engine Service	Transmission Service	Power Steering Service	Radiator Service	Cost	Autoshop
		Details:																		
		Details:																		
		Details:																		
		Details:																		
		Details:																		
		Details:																		
		Details:																		
		Details:																		
		Details:																		
		Details:																		
		Details:																		
		Details:																		
		Details:																		

Date	ODO	Oil Change	Rotate Tires	Replace Tires	Alignment	Cabin Air Filter	Engine Air Filter	Wiper Blades	Headlights / Taillights	Spark Plugs	BATTERY	Belts & Hoses	Brake Service	Suspension Service	Engine Service	Transmission Service	Power Steering Service	Radiator Service	Cost	Autoshop
		Details:																		
		Details:																		
		Details:																		
		Details:																		
		Details:																		
		Details:																		
		Details:																		
		Details:																		
		Details:																		
		Details:																		
		Details:																		
		Details:																		
		Details:																		

Date	ODO	Oil Change	Rotate Tires	Replace Tires	Alignment	Cabin Air Filter	Engine Air Filter	Wiper Blades	Headlights / Taillights	Spark Plugs	BATTERY	Belts & Hoses	Brake Service	Suspension Service	Engine Service	Transmission Service	Power Steering Service	Radiator Service	Cost	Autoshop
		Details:																		
		Details:																		
		Details:																		
		Details:																		
		Details:																		
		Details:																		
		Details:																		
		Details:																		
		Details:																		
		Details:																		
		Details:																		
		Details:																		
		Details:																		

Date	ODO	Oil Change	Rotate Tires	Replace Tires	Alignment	Cabin Air Filter	Engine Air Filter	Wiper Blades	Headlights / Taillights	Spark Plugs	BATTERY	Belts & Hoses	Brake Service	Suspension Service	Engine Service	Transmission Service	Power Steering Service	Radiator Service	Cost	Autoshop
		Details:																		
		Details:																		
		Details:																		
		Details:																		
		Details:																		
		Details:																		
		Details:																		
		Details:																		
		Details:																		
		Details:																		
		Details:																		
		Details:																		
		Details:																		

Date	ODO	Oil Change	Rotate Tires	Replace Tires	Alignment	Cabin Air Filter	Engine Air Filter	Wiper Blades	Headlights / Taillights	Spark Plugs	BATTERY	Belts & Hoses	Brake Service	Suspension Service	Engine Service	Transmission Service	Power Steering Service	Radiator Service	Cost	Autoshop
		Details:																		
		Details:																		
		Details:																		
		Details:																		
		Details:																		
		Details:																		
		Details:																		
		Details:																		
		Details:																		
		Details:																		
		Details:																		
		Details:																		
		Details:																		

Date	ODO	Oil Change	Rotate Tires	Replace Tires	Alignment	Cabin Air Filter	Engine Air Filter	Wiper Blades	Headlights / Taillights	Spark Plugs	BATTERY	Belts & Hoses	Brake Service	Suspension Service	Engine Service	Transmission Service	Power Steering Service	Radiator Service	Cost	Autoshop

Details:

Details:

Details:

Details:

Details:

Details:

Details:

Details:

Details:

Details:

Details:

Details:

Details:

Date	ODO	Oil Change	Rotate Tires	Replace Tires	Alignment	Cabin Air Filter	Engine Air Filter	Wiper Blades	Headlights / Taillights	Spark Plugs	BATTERY	Belts & Hoses	Brake Service	Suspension Service	Engine Service	Transmission Service	Power Steering Service	Radiator Service	Cost	Autoshop
Details:																				
Details:																				
Details:																				
Details:																				
Details:																				
Details:																				
Details:																				
Details:																				
Details:																				
Details:																				
Details:																				
Details:																				
Details:																				

Date	ODO	Oil Change	Rotate Tires	Replace Tires	Alignment	Cabin Air Filter	Engine Air Filter	Wiper Blades	Headlights / Taillights	Spark Plugs	BATTERY	Belts & Hoses	Brake Service	Suspension Service	Engine Service	Transmission Service	Power Steering Service	Radiator Service	Cost	Autoshop
		Details:																		
		Details:																		
		Details:																		
		Details:																		
		Details:																		
		Details:																		
		Details:																		
		Details:																		
		Details:																		
		Details:																		
		Details:																		
		Details:																		
		Details:																		

Date	ODO	Oil Change	Rotate Tires	Replace Tires	Alignment	Cabin Air Filter	Engine Air Filter	Wiper Blades	Headlights/Taillights	Spark Plugs	BATTERY	Belts & Hoses	Brake Service	Suspension Service	Engine Service	Transmission Service	Power Steering Service	Radiator Service	Cost	Autoshop
		Details:																		
		Details:																		
		Details:																		
		Details:																		
		Details:																		
		Details:																		
		Details:																		
		Details:																		
		Details:																		
		Details:																		
		Details:																		
		Details:																		
		Details:																		

Date	ODO	Oil Change	Rotate Tires	Replace Tires	Alignment	Cabin Air Filter	Engine Air Filter	Wiper Blades	Headlights / Taillights	Spark Plugs	BATTERY	Belts & Hoses	Brake Service	Suspension Service	Engine Service	Transmission Service	Power Steering Service	Radiator Service	Cost	Autoshop
								Details:												
								Details:												
								Details:												
								Details:												
								Details:												
								Details:												
								Details:												
								Details:												
								Details:												
								Details:												
								Details:												
								Details:												
								Details:												

Date	ODO	Oil Change	Rotate Tires	Replace Tires	Alignment	Cabin Air Filter	Engine Air Filter	Wiper Blades	Headlights / Taillights	Spark Plugs	BATTERY	Belts & Hoses	Brake Service	Suspension Service	Engine Service	Transmission Service	Power Steering Service	Radiator Service	Cost	Autoshop
		Details:																		
		Details:																		
		Details:																		
		Details:																		
		Details:																		
		Details:																		
		Details:																		
		Details:																		
		Details:																		
		Details:																		
		Details:																		
		Details:																		

Date	ODO	Oil Change	Rotate Tires	Replace Tires	Alignment	Cabin Air Filter	Engine Air Filter	Wiper Blades	Headlights / Taillights	Spark Plugs	BATTERY	Belts & Hoses	Brake Service	Suspension Service	Engine Service	Transmission Service	Power Steering Service	Radiator Service	Cost	Autoshop
		Details:																		
		Details:																		
		Details:																		
		Details:																		
		Details:																		
		Details:																		
		Details:																		
		Details:																		
		Details:																		
		Details:																		
		Details:																		
		Details:																		
		Details:																		

Date	ODO	Oil Change	Rotate Tires	Replace Tires	Alignment	Cabin Air Filter	Engine Air Filter	Wiper Blades	Headlights / Taillights	Spark Plugs	BATTERY	Belts & Hoses	Brake Service	Suspension Service	Engine Service	Transmission Service	Power Steering Service	Radiator Service	Cost	Autoshop
		Details:																		
		Details:																		
		Details:																		
		Details:																		
		Details:																		
		Details:																		
		Details:																		
		Details:																		
		Details:																		
		Details:																		
		Details:																		
		Details:																		

Date	ODO	Oil Change	Rotate Tires	Replace Tires	Alignment	Cabin Air Filter	Engine Air Filter	Wiper Blades	Headlights / Taillights	Spark Plugs	BATTERY	Belts & Hoses	Brake Service	Suspension Service	Engine Service	Transmission Service	Power Steering Service	Radiator Service	Cost	Autoshop
		Details:																		
		Details:																		
		Details:																		
		Details:																		
		Details:																		
		Details:																		
		Details:																		
		Details:																		
		Details:																		
		Details:																		
		Details:																		
		Details:																		
		Details:																		

Date	ODO	Oil Change	Rotate Tires	Replace Tires	Alignment	Cabin Air Filter	Engine Air Filter	Wiper Blades	Headlights / Taillights	Spark Plugs	BATTERY	Belts & Hoses	Brake Service	Suspension Service	Engine Service	Transmission Service	Power Steering Service	Radiator Service	Cost	Autoshop
		Details:																		
		Details:																		
		Details:																		
		Details:																		
		Details:																		
		Details:																		
		Details:																		
		Details:																		
		Details:																		
		Details:																		
		Details:																		
		Details:																		
		Details:																		

Date	ODO	Oil Change	Rotate Tires	Replace Tires	Alignment	Cabin Air Filter	Engine Air Filter	Wiper Blades	Headlights / Taillights	Spark Plugs	BATTERY	Belts & Hoses	Brake Service	Suspension Service	Engine Service	Transmission Service	Power Steering Service	Radiator Service	Cost	Autoshop
		Details:																		
		Details:																		
		Details:																		
		Details:																		
		Details:																		
		Details:																		
		Details:																		
		Details:																		
		Details:																		
		Details:																		
		Details:																		
		Details:																		
		Details:																		

Date	ODO	Oil Change	Rotate Tires	Replace Tires	Alignment	Cabin Air Filter	Engine Air Filter	Wiper Blades	Headlights / Taillights	Spark Plugs	BATTERY	Belts & Hoses	Brake Service	Suspension Service	Engine Service	Transmission Service	Power Steering Service	Radiator Service	Cost	Autoshop
		Details:																		
		Details:																		
		Details:																		
		Details:																		
		Details:																		
		Details:																		
		Details:																		
		Details:																		
		Details:																		
		Details:																		
		Details:																		
		Details:																		
		Details:																		

Date	ODO	Oil Change	Rotate Tires	Replace Tires	Alignment	Cabin Air Filter	Engine Air Filter	Wiper Blades	Headlights / Taillights	Spark Plugs	BATTERY	Belts & Hoses	Brake Service	Suspension Service	Engine Service	Transmission Service	Power Steering Service	Radiator Service	Cost	Autoshop
		Details:																		
		Details:																		
		Details:																		
		Details:																		
		Details:																		
		Details:																		
		Details:																		
		Details:																		
		Details:																		
		Details:																		
		Details:																		
		Details:																		

Date	ODO	Oil Change	Rotate Tires	Replace Tires	Alignment	Cabin Air Filter	Engine Air Filter	Wiper Blades	Headlights / Taillights	Spark Plugs	BATTERY	Belts & Hoses	Brake Service	Suspension Service	Engine Service	Transmission Service	Power Steering Service	Radiator Service	Cost	Autoshop
		Details:																		
		Details:																		
		Details:																		
		Details:																		
		Details:																		
		Details:																		
		Details:																		
		Details:																		
		Details:																		
		Details:																		
		Details:																		
		Details:																		
		Details:																		

Date	ODO	Oil Change	Rotate Tires	Replace Tires	Alignment	Cabin Air Filter	Engine Air Filter	Wiper Blades	Headlights / Taillights	Spark Plugs	BATTERY	Belts & Hoses	Brake Service	Suspension Service	Engine Service	Transmission Service	Power Steering Service	Radiator Service	Cost	Autoshop
		Details:																		
		Details:																		
		Details:																		
		Details:																		
		Details:																		
		Details:																		
		Details:																		
		Details:																		
		Details:																		
		Details:																		
		Details:																		
		Details:																		
		Details:																		

Date	ODO	Oil Change	Rotate Tires	Replace Tires	Alignment	Cabin Air Filter	Engine Air Filter	Wiper Blades	Headlights / Taillights	Spark Plugs	BATTERY	Belts & Hoses	Brake Service	Suspension Service	Engine Service	Transmission Service	Power Steering Service	Radiator Service	Cost	Autoshop
		Details:																		
		Details:																		
		Details:																		
		Details:																		
		Details:																		
		Details:																		
		Details:																		
		Details:																		
		Details:																		
		Details:																		
		Details:																		
		Details:																		

Date	ODO	Oil Change	Rotate Tires	Replace Tires	Alignment	Cabin Air Filter	Engine Air Filter	Wiper Blades	Headlights / Taillights	Spark Plugs	BATTERY	Belts & Hoses	Brake Service	Suspension Service	Engine Service	Transmission Service	Power Steering Service	Radiator Service	Cost	Autoshop
		Details:																		
		Details:																		
		Details:																		
		Details:																		
		Details:																		
		Details:																		
		Details:																		
		Details:																		
		Details:																		
		Details:																		
		Details:																		
		Details:																		
		Details:																		

Date	ODO	Oil Change	Rotate Tires	Replace Tires	Alignment	Cabin Air Filter	Engine Air Filter	Wiper Blades	Headlights / Taillights	Spark Plugs	BATTERY	Belts & Hoses	Brake Service	Suspension Service	Engine Service	Transmission Service	Power Steering Service	Radiator Service	Cost	Autoshop
		Details:																		
		Details:																		
		Details:																		
		Details:																		
		Details:																		
		Details:																		
		Details:																		
		Details:																		
		Details:																		
		Details:																		
		Details:																		
		Details:																		
		Details:																		

Date	ODO	Oil Change	Rotate Tires	Replace Tires	Alignment	Cabin Air Filter	Engine Air Filter	Wiper Blades	Headlights / Taillights	Spark Plugs	BATTERY	Belts & Hoses	Brake Service	Suspension Service	Engine Service	Transmission Service	Power Steering Service	Radiator Service	Cost	Autoshop
		Details:																		
		Details:																		
		Details:																		
		Details:																		
		Details:																		
		Details:																		
		Details:																		
		Details:																		
		Details:																		
		Details:																		
		Details:																		
		Details:																		
		Details:																		

Date	ODO	Oil Change	Rotate Tires	Replace Tires	Alignment	Cabin Air Filter	Engine Air Filter	Wiper Blades	Headlights / Taillights	Spark Plugs	BATTERY	Belts & Hoses	Brake Service	Suspension Service	Engine Service	Transmission Service	Power Steering Service	Radiator Service	Cost	Autoshop
		Details:																		
		Details:																		
		Details:																		
		Details:																		
		Details:																		
		Details:																		
		Details:																		
		Details:																		
		Details:																		
		Details:																		
		Details:																		
		Details:																		
		Details:																		

Date	ODO	Oil Change	Rotate Tires	Replace Tires	Alignment	Cabin Air Filter	Engine Air Filter	Wiper Blades	Headlights / Taillights	Spark Plugs	BATTERY	Belts & Hoses	Brake Service	Suspension Service	Engine Service	Transmission Service	Power Steering Service	Radiator Service	Cost	Autoshop
		Details:																		
		Details:																		
		Details:																		
		Details:																		
		Details:																		
		Details:																		
		Details:																		
		Details:																		
		Details:																		
		Details:																		
		Details:																		
		Details:																		
		Details:																		

Date	ODO	Oil Change	Rotate Tires	Replace Tires	Alignment	Cabin Air Filter	Engine Air Filter	Wiper Blades	Headlights / Taillights	Spark Plugs	BATTERY	Belts & Hoses	Brake Service	Suspension Service	Engine Service	Transmission Service	Power Steering Service	Radiator Service	Cost	Autoshop
Details:																				
Details:																				
Details:																				
Details:																				
Details:																				
Details:																				
Details:																				
Details:																				
Details:																				
Details:																				
Details:																				
Details:																				

Date	ODO	Oil Change	Rotate Tires	Replace Tires	Alignment	Cabin Air Filter	Engine Air Filter	Wiper Blades	Headlights / Taillights	Spark Plugs	BATTERY	Belts & Hoses	Brake Service	Suspension Service	Engine Service	Transmission Service	Power Steering Service	Radiator Service	Cost	Autoshop
		Details:																		
		Details:																		
		Details:																		
		Details:																		
		Details:																		
		Details:																		
		Details:																		
		Details:																		
		Details:																		
		Details:																		
		Details:																		
		Details:																		

Date	ODO	Oil Change	Rotate Tires	Replace Tires	Alignment	Cabin Air Filter	Engine Air Filter	Wiper Blades	Headlights / Taillights	Spark Plugs	BATTERY	Belts & Hoses	Brake Service	Suspension Service	Engine Service	Transmission Service	Power Steering Service	Radiator Service	Cost	Autoshop

Details:

Details:

Details:

Details:

Details:

Details:

Details:

Details:

Details:

Details:

Details:

Details:

Details:

Date	ODO	Oil Change	Rotate Tires	Replace Tires	Alignment	Cabin Air Filter	Engine Air Filter	Wiper Blades	Headlights / Taillights	Spark Plugs	BATTERY	Belts & Hoses	Brake Service	Suspension Service	Engine Service	Transmission Service	Power Steering Service	Radiator Service	Cost	Autoshop
		Details:																		
		Details:																		
		Details:																		
		Details:																		
		Details:																		
		Details:																		
		Details:																		
		Details:																		
		Details:																		
		Details:																		
		Details:																		
		Details:																		
		Details:																		

Date	ODO	Oil Change	Rotate Tires	Replace Tires	Alignment	Cabin Air Filter	Engine Air Filter	Wiper Blades	Headlights / Taillights	Spark Plugs	BATTERY	Belts & Hoses	Brake Service	Suspension Service	Engine Service	Transmission Service	Power Steering Service	Radiator Service	Cost	Autoshop
		Details:																		
		Details:																		
		Details:																		
		Details:																		
		Details:																		
		Details:																		
		Details:																		
		Details:																		
		Details:																		
		Details:																		
		Details:																		
		Details:																		
		Details:																		

Date	ODO	Oil Change	Rotate Tires	Replace Tires	Alignment	Cabin Air Filter	Engine Air Filter	Wiper Blades	Headlights / Taillights	Spark Plugs	BATTERY	Belts & Hoses	Brake Service	Suspension Service	Engine Service	Transmission Service	Power Steering Service	Radiator Service	Cost	Autoshop
		Details:																		
		Details:																		
		Details:																		
		Details:																		
		Details:																		
		Details:																		
		Details:																		
		Details:																		
		Details:																		
		Details:																		
		Details:																		
		Details:																		

Date	ODO	Oil Change	Rotate Tires	Replace Tires	Alignment	Cabin Air Filter	Engine Air Filter	Wiper Blades	Headlights/Taillights	Spark Plugs	BATTERY	Belts & Hoses	Brake Service	Suspension Service	Engine Service	Transmission Service	Power Steering Service	Radiator Service	Cost	Autoshop
Details:																				
Details:																				
Details:																				
Details:																				
Details:																				
Details:																				
Details:																				
Details:																				
Details:																				
Details:																				
Details:																				
Details:																				

Date	ODO	Oil Change	Rotate Tires	Replace Tires	Alignment	Cabin Air Filter	Engine Air Filter	Wiper Blades	Headlights / Taillights	Spark Plugs	BATTERY	Belts & Hoses	Brake Service	Suspension Service	Engine Service	Transmission Service	Power Steering Service	Radiator Service	Cost	Autoshop
		Details:																		
		Details:																		
		Details:																		
		Details:																		
		Details:																		
		Details:																		
		Details:																		
		Details:																		
		Details:																		
		Details:																		
		Details:																		
		Details:																		
		Details:																		

Date	ODO	Oil Change	Rotate Tires	Replace Tires	Alignment	Cabin Air Filter	Engine Air Filter	Wiper Blades	Headlights / Taillights	Spark Plugs	BATTERY	Belts & Hoses	Brake Service	Suspension Service	Engine Service	Transmission Service	Power Steering Service	Radiator Service	Cost	Autoshop
		Details:																		
		Details:																		
		Details:																		
		Details:																		
		Details:																		
		Details:																		
		Details:																		
		Details:																		
		Details:																		
		Details:																		
		Details:																		
		Details:																		
		Details:																		

ACCIDENT CHECKLIST & LOG

STEPS AT THE SCENE

1. Calmly Check for Injuries
If anyone has serious injuries, call for help immediately... if damage is minor, move your vehicle to the side of the road to avoid more accidents

2. Call Police
Discuss incident with officer & ask for a copy of the report

3. Take Photos & Notes
This will help with insurance reporting later. If police do not come due to low severity, use your photos/notes to file a police report at station

4. Exchange information
see section below

AFTERWARDS

5. Contact Your Insurance
Helps avoid false claims against you and makes process smooth

Exchange Information

COLLECT:

Incident Details
- Time: _____
- Date: _____
- Location: _____
- Conditions: _____

- Officer Name: _____
- Badge #: _____
- Police Dept: _____
- Report #: _____

Other Driver Information
- Name: _____
- Phone / Email: _____
- Make & Model: _____
- License Plate: _____
- Insurance Co: _____
- Policy #: _____

WITNESS NAMES & PHONE
(when applicable)

GIVE OUT:
- ☐ Your Name
- ☐ Phone / Email
- ☐ Insurance Carrier
- ☐ Policy Number

OTHER NOTES

ACCIDENT CHECKLIST & LOG

STEPS AT THE SCENE

1. Calmly Check for Injuries
If anyone has serious injuries, call for help immediately... if damage is minor, move your vehicle to the side of the road to avoid more accidents

2. Call Police
Discuss incident with officer & ask for a copy of the report

3. Take Photos & Notes
This will help with insurance reporting later. If police do not come due to low severity, use your photos/notes to file a police report at station

4. Exchange information
see section below

AFTERWARDS

5. Contact Your Insurance
Helps avoid false claims against you and makes process smooth

Exchange Information

COLLECT:

INCIDENT DETAILS
- Time: _____
- Date: _____
- Location: _____
- Conditions: _____

- Officer Name: _____
- Badge #: _____
- Police Dept: _____
- Report #: _____

OTHER DRIVER INFORMATION
- Name: _____
- Phone / Email: _____
- Make & Model: _____
- License Plate: _____
- Insurance Co: _____
- Policy #: _____

WITNESS NAMES & PHONE
(when applicable)

GIVE OUT:
- ☐ Your Name
- ☐ Phone / Email
- ☐ Insurance Carrier
- ☐ Policy Number

OTHER NOTES

ACCIDENT CHECKLIST & LOG

STEPS AT THE SCENE

1. **Calmly Check for Injuries**
   If anyone has serious injuries, call for help immediately... if damage is minor, move your vehicle to the side of the road to avoid more accidents

2. **Call Police**
   Discuss incident with officer & ask for a copy of the report

3. **Take Photos & Notes**
   This will help with insurance reporting later. If police do not come due to low severity, use your photos/notes to file a police report at station

4. **Exchange information**
   see section below

AFTERWARDS

5. **Contact Your Insurance**
   Helps avoid false claims against you and makes process smooth

Exchange Information

COLLECT:

INCIDENT DETAILS
- Time: _____
- Date: _____
- Location: _____
- Conditions: _____

- Officer Name: _____
- Badge #: _____
- Police Dept: _____
- Report #: _____

OTHER DRIVER INFORMATION
- Name: _____
- Phone / Email: _____
- Make & Model: _____
- License Plate: _____
- Insurance Co: _____
- Policy #: _____

WITNESS NAMES & PHONE
(when applicable)

GIVE OUT:
- ☐ Your Name
- ☐ Phone / Email
- ☐ Insurance Carrier
- ☐ Policy Number

OTHER NOTES

ACCIDENT CHECKLIST & LOG

STEPS AT THE SCENE

1. Calmly Check for Injuries
If anyone has serious injuries, call for help immediately... if damage is minor, move your vehicle to the side of the road to avoid more accidents

2. Call Police
Discuss incident with officer & ask for a copy of the report

3. Take Photos & Notes
This will help with insurance reporting later. If police do not come due to low severity, use your photos/notes to file a police report at station

4. Exchange information
see section below

AFTERWARDS

5. Contact Your Insurance
Helps avoid false claims against you and makes process smooth

Exchange Information

COLLECT:

INCIDENT DETAILS
- Time: _____
- Date: _____
- Location: _____
- Conditions: _____

- Officer Name: _____
- Badge #: _____
- Police Dept: _____
- Report #: _____

OTHER DRIVER INFORMATION
- Name: _____
- Phone / Email: _____
- Make & Model: _____
- License Plate: _____
- Insurance Co: _____
- Policy #: _____

WITNESS NAMES & PHONE
(when applicable)

GIVE OUT:
- ☐ Your Name
- ☐ Phone / Email
- ☐ Insurance Carrier
- ☐ Policy Number

OTHER NOTES

ACCIDENT CHECKLIST & LOG

STEPS AT THE SCENE

1. Calmly Check for Injuries
If anyone has serious injuries, call for help immediately... if damage is minor, move your vehicle to the side of the road to avoid more accidents

2. Call Police
Discuss incident with officer & ask for a copy of the report

3. Take Photos & Notes
This will help with insurance reporting later. If police do not come due to low severity, use your photos/notes to file a police report at station

4. Exchange information
see section below

AFTERWARDS

5. Contact Your Insurance
Helps avoid false claims against you and makes process smooth

Exchange Information

COLLECT:

INCIDENT DETAILS
- Time: _____
- Date: _____
- Location: _____
- Conditions: _____

- Officer Name: _____
- Badge #: _____
- Police Dept: _____
- Report #: _____

OTHER DRIVER INFORMATION
- Name: _____
- Phone / Email: _____
- Make & Model: _____
- License Plate: _____
- Insurance Co: _____
- Policy #: _____

WITNESS NAMES & PHONE
(when applicable)

GIVE OUT:
- ☐ Your Name
- ☐ Phone / Email
- ☐ Insurance Carrier
- ☐ Policy Number

OTHER NOTES

Made in the USA
Coppell, TX
29 June 2025

51287542R00066